Let's Do Battle

By
Frank S.

One **Black** Man's
View of
AMERICA

Canadian Cataloguing in Publication Data

S, Frank, 1966-
   Let's do battle
   One black man's view of America

   Includes index.
   ISBN 1-55212-526-2

   1. African Americans--Social conditions. 2. United State
Race relations. I. Title.
E185.86.T84 2000   305.8986'073
C00-911473-4

TRAFFORD

This book was published *on-demand* **in cooperation with Trafford Publishing.**
On-demand publishing is a unique process and service of making a book available for retail
sale to the public taking advantage of on-demand manufacturing and Internet marketing.
On-demand publishing includes promotions, retail sales, manufacturing, order fulfilment,
accounting and collecting royalties on behalf of the author.

Suite 6E, 2333 Government St., Victoria, B.C. V8T 4P4, CANADA

Phone	250-383-6864	Toll-free	1-888-232-4444 (Canada & US)
Fax	250-383-6804	E-mail	sales@trafford.com
Web site	www.trafford.com	TRAFFORD PUBLISHING IS A DIVISION OF TRAFFORD HOLDINGS LTD.	
Trafford Catalogue #00-0191		www.trafford.com/robots/00-0191.html	

10   9   8   7   6

TABLE OF CONTENTS

DEDICATION

DEDICATION

As humans we are often faced with various trials and tribulations in life. Some events make us better for the experience, and others provide us with knowledge for the future. Experience brings useful knowledge, which we can draw upon, later in life. I would like to thank God for allowing me to experience the things in life that can make us stronger. I would like to thank Him for showing me all things happen for a reason, for giving me the strength to make it through these times, both good and bad. I would like to thank Him for showing me the race is not won by the swift, but by the one which endures till the end, for not always making things easy for me and for requiring me to work for every thing I have.

Today I am truly grateful to God for giving me a loving wife, a beautiful son and a supportive family. I am dedicating this book to my wife, Sebrena Tull, and my son, Frank Tull. Sebrena has been supportive of my thoughts of writing this book from day one. From the moment I suggested writing the book, her very words were, "Go ahead". While others told me it was a stupid idea or that there is too much competition, Sebrena said it's worth a try. My wife shares this dedication, with my son Frank S. Tull II. My son Frank was my inspiration while putting the book together. I became even more inspired every time I thought about him and the world ahead of him. Every time I thought about the future that awaits him, and the horrible progress, we have made as people of color, I wrote more. I wrote with the hope that something I wrote might inspire someone to change. I wrote with the hopes that this might create in him a true man. My hope is that he might be the real man we all strive to become.

All proceeds from this book will go to providing a better life for my family and for all that are willing make a change. I will use all available resources to promote change and to support change. I dedicate this book to any and all individuals who are willing to join the fight for change and who are not afraid to make the required sacrifice, all persons who are not fearful of standing up for right no matter how unpopular that stance may be. You have now read the dedication. Please read the whole book.

Special Thanks to:

Logan Tull
Thelma Dougal
Oliver Tull
Bonnie Thompson
Sheneeza Thompson
Frankie Thompson
Golen Thompson

This book written in memory of Dr. Frank William Thompson
(Go Cowboys)

1.

Meet The Enemy

In order for this book to provide you with the vision to go forward, it is vital for the reader to open his or her mind. My hope is that by the end of this work, that you will realize the view through two black eyes is very different from that of mainstream America. Our experience and exposure, combined with restricted growth has created a new being. Black Americans can only change their condition through a new commitment to go to war. The experiences of slavery and segregation just cannot be over looked or downplayed. These are circumstances that cause a true breakdown in the mentality of a race. In order to do battle, we must first establish whom the enemy, or our source of combat will be. Fifty years ago black Americans were requested by the United States army to join in the battle to protect the freedom, and democracy of all Americans in World War II. This request came in the form of the draft during a time when black Americans were not being treated as Americans. Freedom and democracy were mere words that did not apply to all. For blacks the word enemy had various levels of meaning. The enemy came in the form of America through racism and in the form of a shared enemy of the United States in battle. Today our enemies still come in two forms. When you look at our history the enemy is brought into focus. Recently black filmmakers have tried to recreate some of the battles. Recently there was a movie made about the story of Rosewood. A small town composed of blacks that was torn down and set on fire, and many of the citizens were murdered. The movie with the same title was made to tell the story based on eyewitness accounts from that time. Witnesses stated that the Knights of the Ku Klux Klan carried out the murders. Rosewood was a moment in time, but time goes on. In July of 1998 the Southern Poverty Law Center won a big financial verdict against South Carolina's Christian Knights of the Ku Klux Klan for burning a black church (SPC newsletter 2-1999). In issues dealing with the Klan it is very easy to establish who the enemy is. For the Southern Poverty Law Center the enemy was not the Klan, but the chapter known as the South Carolina's Christian Knights. Recent history has shown us the reality of racism and its presence. As we hear of stories like that of Susan Smith who cried wolf. She boasted a grim story of her children being taken by a black man. She knew by stating the color of the car jackers she would gain immediate support from white America against the enemy. The minute the story was told it was quite obvious that she was right. Lynch mobs began to form to find this black man. Thank God no one was around to fit the description. Stories like these should serve as constant reminders to all people, especially people of color of how far we have to go. With recent advancements within the work place, schools and housing we as people of color have been lulled into a condition of contentment. We have begun to see ourselves as equal with equal opportunity to that of our white counterparts. Sometimes how you see yourself is not enough to succeed. How others view you can be vital to your progress as well.

Webster's dictionary (1998 addition) defines free as "not

restricted, controlled, or compelled by another; independent. Not hindered or weighted down as by debt or obligations, having full option. " The fact of the matter is we have come along way, but we have gone nowhere in the last 20 years. We are far from having the freedom described by Webster. This definition however was written through the eyes of a white man. This definition explains what freedom means to a white man. We as blacks are still not free in America. We still are former slaves working towards our freedom. We must continue to work to maintain, and to obtain freedom. We have aloud ourselves to rest on the works of others who came before us, we are constantly looking for someone else to do the work which may have been intended for us. I believe the great leaders of the past would be ashamed of the inability of our people to pick up the torch and run to the next level, our inability to pass the need to progress and continue the move forward on to our children. We have no one but ourselves to blame for the fact our kids are unprepared to compete on any field, which does not require athletic ability. Our worst fears have developed into reality. We have spotted the enemy and we are it.

We are underrepresented in the areas of science, math and English in a world where these skills are paramount. We depend on other races for all items of importance, from toilet paper to towels. With so many of us spending money yearly, it would seem only logical that we should benefit from our own spending, but the opposite is true. We manufacture nothing and own even less. We have taken our black colleges and turned them into second class institutions for those who could not attend the white school of their choice. We have made the white schools rich with our greatest athletes while the black schools struggle for attendance.

We can say what we choose about white America, but one thing is true. As a group white Americans are not afraid to take chances and create opportunity for themselves. White Americans support their own endeavors and give to their own communities. White Americans have a lot to be proud of when it comes to accomplishments. White Americans have a clear understanding of self, and realize the importance of history in relation to the future progress of white Americans. Black America must adopt this mentality.

Black American's are in need of reconstruction from the ground up, starting with the purpose of the black man, and focusing on the mentality of the black woman. The reconstruction must stem deep into the hearts of our children, and extend across generational lines to reach their children as well. We can never change the views of others towards us until we change our views of ourselves. **Right now, because of our actions, reactions, and often lack of action, we have become our own worst enemy.**

We have allowed ourselves to stray away from the true things in life which are important, and we have begun to suffer for it. Family, education, vision and individual respect are the basic elements of the progress of a people. We are suffering and will continue to suffer until we make the conscious choice to change. This change, although government and whites can assist the change, the transformation cannot be made solely by them. This change must begin with the black man and be shared by the black woman and adopted by the black child. This manual will encourage you as a person of color to look within yourself, and the resources that are yours, to find relief. Ask yourself, what can I do today to change my situation? This book will request that the white individual dig within their souls to find truth. They should find the real truth and not the truth they find comforting. It's time for war and I am not afraid to fire the first shot!

2.

WHO'S THE MAN?

Somewhere along the way the black man has lost his place within the family and society. Many choose to blame this on slavery and the system, which the white man set up. The system gave the slave master power and the position of lord over the black man's wife and his home. Others point to the early days of segregation in which the black man, due to fear of repercussions from the white man, would allow him to do as he pleased with his family. White men would have sex with his wife while he stood outside the door, and then on the way out would say she was all right. Or some feel the periods of war in which large numbers of black men were sent to fight, leaving the woman as the leader of the family, caused the family to function without the black man. Since that day the man has never been able to overcome the positioning of the women.

Well, no matter what nail you choose to hang your hat on, the fact of the matter is we are here and something must be done. Many scholars choose to dwell on the reasons and never on the solution; many men want to write excuses in the sand instead of devising a plan. Our ancestors were the sons of kings and queens, but we are the sons of field hands and house nigger's. Now is the time to admit our past and face the future. As former slaves, we must remember how it felt to have another man tell you to bow before him or be beat.

As former slaves, we must savor the anger we felt as our wives were raped and children killed. We must hold on to the mental picture we took of our mothers and fathers being hung before us while the white man posed for the picture, we must remember how it felt to not be called a man, but a boy. Black men now is the time for the sons of former slaves to rise up and take control of our future. We must use the pain and experience of the past to fuel our drive for the future. The reason we have allowed ourselves to fall into the horrible state we find ourselves in today is because we have forgotten. We have forgotten what our forefathers went through and why it is truly a blessing and an honor to be a black man today.

As black men we must take back our place within the home which was removed from our forefathers when they transitioned from royalty to slavery. We must repaint the picture of ourselves to our women, women who have seen us degraded, beaten down and overlooked. These are women who have felt the need to protect themselves because we could not. We must paint the picture of a king over the picture of a slave, but we cannot have someone else do it for us. We must paint our own picture using the brushes God has supplied. Right now you must evaluate your place within your home. Look at the status of your marriage from your wife's point of view, not yours, and of your status as a father from your kid's point of view. Do not expect things to change right away with your Family. You cannot go into your home today beating on your chest, yelling, "I'm the man and expect everyone to fall in line". The best way to start the transformation is to evaluate your status with your family and friends. Ask each of them to write down what they feel a husband, father or a friend should be, then ask them to write down what they think you are. When they give the feedback, take everything they have said without being critical, keeping in mind that perception is reality. How they see you is how you are, not whom you think your are or how you see yourself. Study the list, taking a good hard look at yourself and your life thus far. From this list, devise a plan for change.

When God gave direction to the Jews, he gave Moses the Ten Commandments to serve as a guide to lead them to the goal of salvation. Your goal is to become the best man you can be using the tools that God has given you. Put together a list of Ten Commandments for yourself to help you reach your goal. This list should be used in addition to the Ten Commandments of God and not in place of. This list will be different for everyone because we all have different needs and sources of inspiration. However if you can't think of any laws for yourself, then you can use mine.
My list is composed of ten sayings, which I have either heard or seen in my life from various sources. I look at this list for inspiration when I'm down and for guidance when I am lost. It gives me strength when I am weak and it reminds me of my goal to be the best man I can be.

I call my list the Ten Laws of Tull. I feel it is very important to name the list because it gives it some identity. Think about who you want to become and where you want to go, and name your list.

The Ten Laws of Tull

1. Believe in God

2. That which does not kill me will make me stronger

3. God has lent you this body and these skills — what you do with them is up to you

4. Learn something new every day

5. You only truly lose if you let them win, so never ever give up

6. Take care of the little things and the big things will take care of themselves

7. Work hard today, but plan for tomorrow

8. You are only as good as tomorrow's performance

9. Never underestimate your opponent

10. You can overcome any situation or setback

These laws will help remind you of the man you want to be, so remember to use things, which will inspire you. Just as we can read the bible for guidance, strength and insight, these laws should each mean something to you personally. It took me twenty-five years to come up with the Ten Laws of Tull and each one has a story and a reason for importance.

1.   Believe in God — When I was younger, I thought I believed in God and that I had favor in his sight until the

devil showed me different. When things really got rough in my life and God removed the protective hedge that he had placed around me, the devil showed me things, I never thought I would see. He also showed me the true Frank S. Tull Sr.

I was the man who looked to himself to make things right without help from anyone (includes God). Oh yes, I said, thank you Lord, often and read the bible, but when things were tough I had no faith. Day in and day out I attempted to solve the problem all by myself. These three words-believe in God - remind me to put my faith in God and to remember that He is always there for me.

2.   That which does not kill me will make me stronger—I adopted this saying in college when I pledged Kappa Alpha Psi (old school) in the middle of two-a-day practices for football while taking classes. I have never gone through more or been made to feel any worse in my life. There were weeks where I went without sleep for three days and still had to practice, go to class and pledge at late night sessions. Today, when things present themselves, I read this line and remember I am stronger because of what I have been through and if this does not kill me (which most things won't), I will be stronger for the experience.

3.   God has lent you this body and these skills, so what you do with them is up to you. God is watching each and every one of us daily to see what we will make of His creation. These laws are the reason why I don't drink, smoke or do drugs. This law is really powerful because when I want to do nothing or be nothing, I remember it and get back on the road to success. ASK YOURSELF, "WHERE AM I NOW AND WHAT AM I DOING WITH HIS CREATION?"

4.   Learn something-new everyday —This line is intended to keep me from getting comfortable with whom I am or what I think I know. We all have more to learn about our selves, and we must be willing to listen and learn from all available sources. My largest sources of knowledge are the bible and my family.

5.   You only lose if you let them win— All black men who are on welfare, unless they are disabled, should remember this. There is always a way and a way out if you just keep looking for it. Too many of us have lost because we gave up too soon. I use this law often to deal with the challenges of my job. When you think you have done everything you can do or said everything you can say, remember this— you haven't.

6.   Take care of the little things and the big things will take care of themselves— As I look forward in life to the goals I would like to accomplish. I use this phrase to remind me to pay attention to detail and to handle the day-to-day requirements, which will build the foundation for attainment of the goal itself in the future. We want a better job, but we don't want to go back to school to get the education we need. Nothing worth having is easy, so you must do the little things. If your goal is to be a good father, you must first hug your kids and spend some time with your wife.

7.   Work hard today, but plan for tomorrow— My mother worked very hard for all of her 75 years of life. She sometimes held as many as three jobs. Every memory I have of her involves her working in some form or fashion. I want to work today so I won't have to work forever. I have a plan for tomorrow which will lead me to a golf course in Florida at the

age of 55.

8.   You are only as good as your next performance—Just because you have done well today does not mean you will do well tomorrow. You must continue to strive to do the best every day. They remember today's performance, not last week's. I think of this every time I get my wife a birthday gift.

9.   Never underestimate your opponent—In every situation there is an opponent of some sort. I look for that opponent and never take my eyes off of it. It may be the test I'm about to take for my job, the message which hides itself in music, the neighbor with the great legs or the best friend who visits when you're not there, but your wife is. Always keep your eyes open. We as black people have not identified our opponents (drugs, music and ourselves) and thus cannot overcome them.

10.   You can overcome any situation or set back—When I want to give up or it seems like things are just way too tough I read this and put it together with #1 and I realize I will be O.K.

If any change is going to occur, it must begin with the black man himself and be carried out by the same. Men, we must form the plan ourselves and stop blaming the white man, the black woman, the government or the past. No matter, who is to blame for the crime, we are the victims who suffer. No longer can we afford to lick our wounds and feel sorry for ourselves. We must take action by getting control of ourselves and putting an end to all things that may hold us back. We must control such items as alcohol, drugs, cigarettes and our music.

Number 9 in the Ten Laws of Tull is never underestimate your opponent, and we have underestimated the effects of all of the above. When the white men came to America, they used alcohol and cigarettes to weaken the minds of the Indian to the true effects of the white man. Indians were so addicted to these drugs they were willing to trade all they had to fulfill their addictions. Today we are trading all that we own, just as the Indians did, for the same drugs. We have underestimated cigarettes and now they eat us from within in the form of cancer, bronchitis, asthma and other forms of lung disease. Alcohol has provided us with the high we have needed to overlook its true effects on our livers and kidneys. The ease of going to the store down the street for a drink has blinded us to the winos in the walkways, the beer bottles in the streets, and the liquor stores on every street corner. These stores provide us with the vice but do nothing for our communities or our children. Drugs continue to squeeze the life from our neighborhoods, robbing us all of the safety we use to feel and the closeness that once existed. Our children are bombarded by this threat daily by forceful drug dealers who will not take no for an answer. We ignore all of this because the true effects of these drugs have not hit us yet.

As black men we must put aside all of these negative vices and focus on the purpose of becoming a new creature. This new creature provides for his family and leads them as a husband and a father, is admired by his friends and respected by his enemies. This new creature is controlled only by God and not by the drugs and desires of man. The white man controlled the Indians with smoke and violence, and now he owns you in the same manner. Stop wasting time perfecting the things of unimportance in life. We have the latest jeans, the most stylish shoes and never miss a week at the barbershop, but our minds are unattended and our bank accounts empty. The things that are truly important, are those things, which last. A new car will be an old car in five years, yet we spend years planning to get the car and then we purchase a Mercedes or a BMW. Because we make a Yugo salary, we are always in debt. We **rent** homes, incurring the costs of water, gas, electricity, trash pick up and basic home maintenance just so we can say we have a home. The truth of the matter is you still do not have a home. Someone else has a home and you are the fool who is paying to maintain it until they want it back. And when that day comes, you will be further back then when you started.

The proper way is to get an apartment paying the least amount of rent you can while still living in a comfortable area. This will allow you to save money for the future and for a home of your own. You can take the money, which is spent painting the garage, or for trash pick up and gas, or lawn maintenance, and put it into the savings account for a new home. Become a man of your word. Make your word mean something, not just to yourself, but to everyone else. Before you agree to anything, think hard about it to make sure it is something that you can actually do. For so long we have said without thought, "Oh yes, I will do that" "No problem, I will be there," when in reality we knew we either could not do it or really did not want to. These situations, combined with the other times when we just flat-out lied, have given our women, children and friends good reason to not expect us to keep our word.

You must make the change occur through example.

Every time your girl asks you to do something, think before you answer. If she wants to go to dinner on Thursday and Thursday is the day you planned to play ball at the gym with the boys, tell her this. "Honey, I would love to take you to dinner on Thursday, but I already made plans to play basketball. Would it be O.K. if we went on Wednesday or Friday? This will allow her to still go to dinner and allow you to still play ball without anyone getting mad or in trouble. The problem is, we don't do this. We say O.K. to the Thursday dinner and then we try to go play ball, get home take a shower and pick up our girl for dinner prior to the dinner reservations. We end up losing track of time and either picking up our girl one hour late or getting caught in traffic, missing the dinner altogether. No matter what the result, our baby is mad and she ends up going off. From the start, be up front with your girl no matter what her status is — girlfriend or wife. A woman will respect you more if she knows what you say is what you will do and if you can't do it you won't say it. Being a man of your word takes on an even more intense meaning when kids are involved. A child hears and records everything and promises are heard at twelve times the normal pitch to insure they are not forgotten. When you tell your child something, re-member — they will expect it to happen.

If you tell your child you will take them to the zoo, you should already have planned the date, time and location prior to even asking them to go. The minute you say, "how would you like to go?" they will ask you when and where and will expect it to happen on those dates and times. Make sure you write it down and do not have anything else planned. If you invited your child and told them it would be just the tow of you, do not invite anyone else. Remember that they know you did not say that Keshawn (Kee-shunn) was coming along, so if

Keshawn shows up they will feel betrayed (especially if you have a daughter). So make sure you make it just you and your child. Now if you would like to improve the relationship between the child and Keshawn if you have kids from another women or if you would like to include mommy make sure to state this up front to the child when the outing is planned. Kids just want their father to be trustworthy and a man of his word all the time. As men, we must become a symbol of honesty and trust worthiness to our families, but it will not come without effort. It must be earned by the kids and proven to your women. Black women have seen so much and been treated so badly they expect the worst and are surprised by the best. We must change that by constantly showing her the best until this is all she knows from us and will eventually only expect more of the same.

Stop wasting time attempting to portray an image and focus on establishing a new identity based on truth. We all know there is very little. The black man owns, controls, or runs, so stop attempting to portray a false image. Only that which is real will last in life and death. As we continue to over extend our boundaries with clothes and material possessions, we fall farther and farther behind in the areas that count. Black brothers, your competition is not the other black man (surprise) — oh no your competition is the mentality of others and the perception you have of yourself. Although the fact that we are still not given equal opportunity to the majority of jobs which exist, or fair housing, car loans, housing loans and offices which require election, these things are a small part of the problem. These obstacles are not the true heart of the problem any more. The true heart of the problem lies within the black man. This heart is what overcame the shackles of slavery and the robes of the KKK. This heart is what allowed us to move from the back of the bus to the corporate office of the bus company, but this heart is also the one which beats more intensely as the trigger is pulled on the gun which is pointed at the heart of another brother. This heart also pumps the cocaine, crack and heroin throughout the body, but most importantly, this is the heart, which gives strength to the mind that chooses to destroy a black women and her kids.

We must regain control of our hearts and start to feel again. We need to shake off this feeling of numbness that has caused us to stand by and watch as things go increasingly wrong and the future becomes bleaker.

Men, it all begins with us and it all begins now. Stop listening to those women's lib groups, who want you to believe you're a fool to request the position of head of your home. Every partnership has a leader, either in the form of a president, CEO, coach or controlling interest group. Well, a relationship is a partnership. In fact, a marriage is the greatest partnership of all because it occurs under God. Because you are the leader of your home, does that make you smarter or stronger or wiser? **Of course you're not stronger or wiser because your male.**

It has always amazed me how in America we come to a pastor or religious figure to receive pre-marital counseling, then go to a church to be married and then have a minister perform the ceremony, but we don't want to follow God's laws in our marriages. If you do not believe in God that's fine, but don't use the church or the minister for the ceremony. God has created the man and women with the intent of enhancing each other. By filling in the gaps, which are created by our flaws and shortcomings, we complete each other. Some special interest groups will tell you that the days of the dominant male are gone with the cave man, but the opposite is true. We need this presence more than ever in our homes as well as our neighborhoods and in society. Remember that you do not have to be dominating to be dominant in the home or the relationship. You can become a dominant figure first by providing your presence within the home as a stable rock for all to depend on.

Spend time with the kids, especially your sons. The downfall of the first generation of blacks after slavery was they were so consumed with saving their own butts and avoiding trouble, they never instilled the pride of a man within their own sons. They never told them, "Even though I am bowing and calling the white man "sir", you must prepare yourself in such a manner so that you will not have to do this." This was their ultimate goal and they should have passed it on. Today, we are no better off mentally than our forefathers were. By allowing the past to be swept under the rug like lint, we turn our backs on the greatest source of strength available. Our young people have no true understanding of the sacrifices that were made for them in the past. They don't realize how vital education and family is to a people. We must educate them on where we have been so they will be glad that they are here instead of there. Now we as black men must end this cycle by spending time with our sons. Tell them you love them and show them what to expect and demand from the future. Focus on your daughters by creating in them a sense of pride, which will allow them to decide for themselves that any dress which reveals more than it covers is not a dress. Help your daughter to see she can control how men and people view her by her dress and actions. As men we realize that in order to be seen as a professional, we must conduct ourselves in a professional manner. Many women feel you should overlook the fact they have their breasts hanging out and something tight on their backside to see the true professional women. Well brother, it is your job to show your young daughter that the mentality of a man is very different from her own, and the respect she gets must be established. The days of the man treating a lady like a lady just because she is a lady, I am sad to say are gone.

Provide your wife with a steady shoulder to lean on in rough times and arms to hold in good ones. Show her the strength that comes from a strong mate and the knowledge, which grows as two heads work together as one. Remember you do not have to be domineering to be dominant. Never use force, and never intimidate your women with threats of violence because she will not respect you; she will simply fear you. Give her good reason to follow your lead, because no one will follow a fool. The black woman wants a man she can feel good about following and feel safe about being with. Prove it to her that you are the man. Black women are calling for a real man, and our children are crying for real fathers. They are begging for someone to step up to be the guiding force, which will lead them, our kids and our people to the life, which God has intended for us all. The true question is "Are you man enough to provide it?"

3.

THERE IS ONLY ONE GOOD WHITE PERSON

Today I am sitting in a restaurant eating lunch with a good friend of mine named Stanley (the name has been changed to protect the innocent). Stanley lives in a small West Texas town outside of Dallas. He is a great guy who says his main stance is that all people should be treated equally no matter what color they are. He likes to say that he does not have a prejudice bone in his body. Although he does call me friend to my face, he is not able to discuss our friendship with some of his friends. In this town the races are very separate and it is not uncommon for the KKK to meet late at night in the woods. In fact Stanley has told me that some of his friends belong to white supremacists groups and have shown support for the skinheads. Although I believe Stanley when he says that he could not care what color I am. I have to wonder what effect his relationship with his friends has on his perception of me. His friends drive the stereotypical southern pick up trucks with the confederate flag on the back. They chew tobacco and have no problem using the words coon or nigger. Right now Stanley is in the middle, but at some point I think he will have to choose a side. In fact by not telling his friends about me he may have already chosen. Within our society we have divided up into teams. These teams have been based on the wrong things and maintained for the wrong reasons. Pay attention the next time you go to an activity that involves persons of different races. One thing you will notice is if there are more than ten of the minority, they will all be together — and so will the whites, which are normally, the majority. In the corporate world, blacks have realized when to and when not to hang. If there are less than ten of us and they see us together, they feel threatened. They wonder why are they not being social by mingling with the white members of the corporation. What they don't realize is they are not talking to us either. In fact, they are on their team talking with their teammates — the other white co-workers.

This color-conscious reality, which has been established by whites and maintained by blacks, has leaked over into every other aspect of our world. A good example of this is the criminal world. When a white person is on trial for a crime, other whites (unless his crime was against other whites) are quick to rush to his defense. The same holds true for blacks. No matter what the evidence looks like, (O.J. Simpson) we want to assume they did not do it or they are just being set up. The fact of the matter is, we are protecting our teammates. We know if he or she is found guilty, it makes the team look bad. Every time one of us goes to jail, the great Gods of the game take one point from us and give it to the white man. Just like every time one of us gets off, the whites lose a point to us. That's why the prosecution was so dead set on getting O.J. in the civil trial. They had to get the point back. How can a man not be found guilty in a court of law and still have to pay damages for his involvement with the death of two people they don't know he killed? Then he has to pay fees greater then he has the potential to earn. See they had to fix that Negro for taking one of their own. There was no way he was going to kill her and get away with it. I realize they say they only want justice. Well, if they wanted justice, they would not want to take away the ability of a man to take care of and provide for his children based on, it sure looked like he did it. My stance is that it is up to the courts to decide if a man is guilty or innocent. If the courts say that there is not enough evidence to convict the man than leave him alone until you find more proof.

No matter what, they have never proven O.J. to be a bad father. He has never brought harm to the kids, so at least allow him to provide for them. Well I guess the O.J. story is another book by itself, but I do reserve the right to reference it later. Today, look at the death of the little girl named JonBenet Ramsey. There is as much evidence against her parents as there was against Mr. Simpson. Their actions are as questionable as his, but white America is not forming a lynch mob for them. The Denver police held higher standards for action for the Ramsey family than the California police did for Mr. Simpson. Craig Silverman a former Denver prosecutor stated that "the district attorney applied too high a standard of proof-beyond a reasonable doubt rather than the probable cause generally required for an indictment" (USA Today Oct 14,1999). The child was murdered in her own home while her parents were there. The evidence did not exclude them yet they are not being booed out of restaurants and banned from neighborhoods. They are being viewed as innocent until proven guilty. Innocent until proven guilty? That's a novel concept. Mr. Simpson was placed on trial for over a year. The city utilized all of its resources to find evidence to convict him, and yet he was not found guilty after a trial. Not found guilty after a trial, yet viewed as guilty by society. The Ramsey's are viewed as innocent until proven guilty without a trial. America needs to stop lying to itself and face the racist music. My point with O.J. is there was no way that he was going to walk away Scot-free. In the eyes of white America, he was guilty, and until he paid in some way they were not going to stop. Maybe that's why blacks won't except the topic of slavery as being over and done. Maybe the evidence was just too great and the pain too deep; we wanted whites to receive some punishment. White's felt O.J. should suffer and they would not rest until he did. It seems to me if this is the case, then we should be able to go back and force the families of former slave owners to pay damages. All blacks should file some sort of joint lawsuit. This lawsuit would involve only the families of those whites (proof would be easy to produce) who killed blacks in slavery and hung blacks during segregation. The suit would force them to pay damages to the families of those black men and women who are gone.

The KKK should be in court right now for all of the death, fear and financial turmoil they have caused to blacks and Jewish people. Between the years of 1885 and 1900, at least 2,500 blacks were lynched or murdered by the KKK (*Newsweek Magazine*, December 8, 1997). Do you want us to believe that there is no way to find out who belonged to the KKK during those time periods? What about who belongs today? Yes, the Klan has lost some token cases such as Mobile, Alabama in 1981 and Portland, Oregon in 1990. Both of these cases ended in judgments totaling around $20-million dollars (SPL Newsletter, 1999). For the death and restructuring of life that has resulted from the Klan they should be forced to disband. Every organization has a role and a list of members. The Klan will never be held fully accountable because they are on the right team. Their team has the courts and the jails on its side. Their team has the highest court in the land on its side. Most importantly, it has the white people on its side simply by association. What we don't realize is as Dr. Martin Luther said, "Non cooperation with evil is as important as cooperation with good". In other words, silence means consent. There are so many good white folks out there who, because of the ways that the teams were divided, ended up in the middle. The fact of the matter is we need to divide the teams up again based on right and wrong and not on color. Stanley should not be in the middle of the war. Stanley should tell his friends that they are wrong and that they should re-look at their view of black people.

There is only one good white person in this world, and it's the one who wants to do right. If you really believe in right then you won't stand by and watch as wrong activity takes place. If you are a schoolteacher and you know a black child is being singled out as a troublemaker, simply because he does not fit the mold of the traditional student, then it is your duty to take a stand. If you are a police officer, and you know your partner handles blacks with more aggression than whites when performing an arrest, then it is your duty to take a stand.

If you are a manager in an apartment complex and you know they are telling blacks they are not leasing, yet are renting to whites, then you must take a stand. If you are a judge and you know of other judges who give unfair sentences to blacks as opposed to whites, then you must take a stand. So often I hear white people say, "I consider myself to be a good person." Well, non-cooperation with evil is as vital as cooperation with good. There is only one good white person in this world, and it's the one who is willing to say, "no more!" The reason we are no longer slaves today is because many whites were willing to go against the system and stand up.

Willing to fight not so much for what was right, but against what was wrong. Many of those who fought in the Civil War on the side of the North really did not like blacks, and in fact thought we should go back to Africa. However, they felt it was wrong to enslave a man for any reason. They fought because they refused to cooperate with evil.

Black folks, we must learn about the importance of standing against wrong also. Just because a person is black gives them no right to steal, sell drugs or murder. Turn them in. There are many methods of stealing I am not just talking about bank robbery. I am talking about that friend of yours who is as healthy as a horse, but because they don't want to work, they are tricking the system to get welfare or disability. I am talking about that house on the corner that everyone in the hood knows about, but won't turn in to the police. Turn them in. I am talking about that nephew-who believes he is hard or tuff and belongs to a gang. In order to show his force, he shows you his bullet wounds and brags about the kids he has killed. That's right, turn that fool in. There are only two types of people no matter what the color — those who want the right thing to occur and do right in their lives, and those who want and do wrong in their lives. If you're not on the side of right, you are the enemy.

4.

I WAS BORN GAY

The 90's have brought about great change for the race known as African Americans. One change that has come is the introduction of gay life as a viable solution. Now more than ever, black men and black women are coming out of the closet, proclaiming their homosexuality. What do these things have in common—prison, murder, disease, white women and Homosexuality? These are all things standing between a black man and a black woman getting married. One would think with all of these forces working to chip away at the small stock of available good men. Homosexuality should have little, if any affect, but the opposite is true. Gay life is worse because it attacks from both sides. Black men are dying and going to jail at an unbelievable rate. Homosexuality removes two men or two women every time it attacks. Although the above is important the most important reason to not support homosexual activity is that it changes the boundaries of that which is considered normal. Recently at a company function I got involved in a conversation with a gay employee and another female sales representative. The first thing that the gay man stated was he was born this way and he can't change the way he feels. All gay and lesbians are gay due to natural reasons and they have no choice. Just as heterosexuals are attracted to one another, so are homosexuals. They are just attracted to the same sex. When I hear this, the first thing that comes to mind is they are absolutely right. Everything they are feeling is dead on target. However, they are not born, nor were they meant to be gay. One thing we must all remember is there are two sides or courses of action for every facet of life. When we are born, we are born with a will and want to do right, and a will and want to do wrong. For everything in this world, the basis for decision is right and wrong. This basis for decision does not require you to believe in God. The basis is neither religiously grounded nor biblically demanding. One does not have to be a Christian to recognize the difference between right and wrong. All that is required is the knowledge to understand, that just because you enjoy doing something does not make it right.

Maybe if I explain it this way it will make more sense. The way in which the black race came to America, and the conditions under which we were assimilated into this country, have created a color-conscious reality which, although we did not support it, we were forced to live with. Earlier I told you about the creation and division of teams—teams based on color. Black vs. White, or Brown, and so on. The truth of the matter is, we should have not paid so much attention to color and focused more on right and wrong. No matter what color you are, if you believe in right, than step over here. If you believe in wrong, then step over there. Since these teams have been divided based on the wrong premise, we now have some players playing on the wrong teams. When a child is born, he is forced to make decisions based on what is right and what is wrong. Many times the feeling to do wrong can be so strong it can be tough to tell which is which. The feeling to do wrong can feel right when fulfilled, yet the action is still wrong. All of us have one thing (at least one) which pulls at us. This one thing may have started in child-hood or maybe high school, but non-the-less it began.

   The feeling to be gay really can begin from birth and it really can feel natural and normal. **The reason why it feels so normal is because the want to do wrong is a normal feeling which we all experience. The difference is who has the strength to over-come the want to do wrong, and re-place it with the will to do right.** I will never forget a certain story, which occurred when I was in the 5th grade. This story was of a child who was only eight years old. Out of jealousy for his baby sister, he took his dad's gun and shot her in the head. At the boy's trial, his father said he had been evil from birth and he wondered if he was a born killer. The fact is, we all have had feelings which were hurtful in origin which fo-cused on bringing harm to others, but we overcame the feel-ing and the want to do wrong. Maybe our thoughts were not of murder, but they were not positive either. This child did not overcome the desire to do wrong. Now more than ever we have heard about children that are molested by adult men. When I talk about the effect on homosexual behavior on that which is considered normal. If you are involved in or support the act of one man having sex with another in the anus, then what position are you in to tell a young man of twenty-two that he should not have sex with a fifteen year old girl. If the girl looks twenty-two, and states that she loves him, then why is it wrong. Especially when you compare it to the action that you partake in. Once again it stretches the boundaries and changes the rules. When a person commits a crime such as murder or rape, society looks at the action as being wrong and we have no problem as a society punishing the person for the action. For some reason the same treatment or view is not applied with the act of homosexuality. When we look at the homosexual we look at the individual who participates in the action, instead of the action they are partaking in. Mothers, fathers and friends have been fooled into believing that in order to except the individual, they have to except their individual actions also. The guy community has presented their sexual actions as if these actions are who they are instead of what they do. Homosexuality is the act of having sex with the same sex. If I choose to stop having sex with women today to have sex only with men, then as of today, I am homosexual. You do not have to abandon your children just because they have participated in an improper action. Judge the action and not the individual. Just because your son who is a great son, a loving father and a fantastic husband commits murder you do not have to stop being his mother. In fact, he is still a great son, a loving father and a fantastic husband. Homosexuality is very similar to the thought process involved with men who commit child molestation. These men often state they have always been attracted to little boys or girls and no they can't control it. Are they any different from the homosexual? Not in the action, because a child does not have the ability to consent, but in the origin of the action. The action just like the act of homosexuality must be denied.

Many lesbian relationships start out with just the two women, but as the relationship continues many of them find themselves implementing outside items to fulfill the bond. Items such as dildos (a sexual device which looks like a penis) or vibrators. **These items simulate the private parts of a man. If the primary attraction of the woman is to the woman as a woman, why would they want to simulate sex with a man?** I believe the lesbian is attracted to the emotional support provided by her partner and the connection they feel as close friends and partners. This substitutes for a true love relationship. The fact of the matter is, it is O.K. to want this emotional uplifting which only a woman can provide for another woman, or to want the compassion a woman's sensitivity offers, but that's what friendships are for. The emotional support gained from the relationship can be fulfilled in friendship without sexual contact. Our relationships are created to provide different areas of fulfillment. Family, friendships and spouses, work together to fulfill each and every need one may have. In marriage a man can do for the woman what no woman (or machine) can do, and the woman can do in marriage what no other man can do.

A trend now has begun within gay relationships to adopt children of heterosexual relationships. Many women, and gay couples say this is a viable option to fulfill their need to be fathers or mothers within the bounds of the homosexual relationship. Earlier I said nothing complete could come from a gay relationship that cannot be found in a heterosexual one. Two men cannot produce children just as two women cannot; however, these persons still have the desire to foster and raise children. Would they have these desires if they were really meant to be gay from birth? Born with the true intent of being with the same sex, then would it not make sense to also be born without the desire to have children? Since there is not a way for them to produce children, why then would they require the desire? A man has the desire to parent, but not the desire to be pregnant. Some might say that no man want's to have a baby due to the pain, but the opposite is true. Some men are jealous of the bond that is created from this experience. I feel a woman becomes closer to God as she helps him to create life through birth. The simple act of touching the stomach by a man does not come close to the joy and trauma experienced by the woman. However, men cannot have children because it's not something we were meant to do. The desire to parent is natural; the act and the relationship are not. These persons must stand up and see the relationship for what it is from the standpoint of right and wrong. The only difference between the gay lifestyle, and the heterosexual lifestyle is the manner in which we have sex. Since this is the only difference despite what you hear, the foundation is a weak one and cannot withstand the tests of time. In fact, if the world were to allow the gays and lesbians to have the U.S. and all heterosexuals went to Africa (I hear it's a wonderful place). In One -Hundred years I can tell you for sure one place which will not require visitation. The only way the homosexuals could survive would be to become bi-sexual. If however, they are able to become bi-sexual out of necessity, then the classification no longer becomes permanent but instead flexible like a choice, and can be classified as a sexual desire instead of a born trait.

For the gay man, the ease of having another man as a partner provides less pressure to perform because when you can't, he can. It also offers less confrontation on the day-to-day activities of life. Most men don't become consumed with the same things as women; most men enjoy doing and watching the same things. Most men understand each other and the need to sometimes be alone. Just as woman have the bond, so do men, but just as it is wrong for women, it is wrong for men. Utilize your friends as friends and if you just feel the need to have anal sex just remember woman have one of those also. The act of sautomy itself is unnatural. A woman's vagina is designed with the ability to generate fluids for intercourse. There are no documented situations of a man's anus generating fluids for intercourse. Without artificial lubrication such as petroleum jelly, anal sex is painful and uncomfortable. I asked one gay man (he would not allow me to use his name) if he were stranded on a desert island with his lover would they continue to have sex. He stated they would have sex twice—once each, but after that neither one of them would subject themselves to such pain. Within the gay community, AIDS spread with great speed and its primary victim was the gay man. AIDS is a blood-based disease primarily spreads by the exchange of body fluids such as semen, saliva and contact with the blood of infected persons (Stedman's Concise Medical Dictionary 2nd edition, 1994). The anus is not designed to accommodate a penis, so when penetration occurs, extreme tearing of tissue takes place. When the tissue is torn, the penis comes in contact with the blood. This is why the gay community suffered from the spread of AIDS at an alarming rate. How natural does that sound?

In the heterosexual union, nothing additional is needed. However, for the gay community, their very existence is in question since they are unable to produce. The greatest thing in the world for a heterosexual relationship is to be stranded on a desert island for a <u>short</u> time with your lover. If you were born to do it, then why should you need artificial lubrication to carry out the act of making love? Brothers and sisters, we need you now to make the right decisions. Choose your team based on right and wrong and not on male or female. Homosexuality is wrong if you look at the purpose of all living creatures including man. Look at the very basis by which we continue to survive. The picture becomes clear that homosexual relationships provide no support to our society, the demands of which are not being met as it is. I am not saying that you will go to hell or that God hates you. To be honest I do not think that the judgment of you is my job. I do think that the bible clearly states that the judgment of your action is my job. God has special blessings for his people here on earth and also awaiting us in heaven. In order for us to obtain the many blessings that God has for us he requires us to keep his commandments. God has commanded us to not commit adultery or fornication. He states through the apostle Paul that "It is good for them to remain even as I am; but if they cannot exercise self-control, let them marry. For it is better to marry than to burn with passion" 1 Corinthians 7:8,9. Over and over again the bible tells us that marriage is a union between a man and woman. Never does it leave room for two men or two women to join in this union under God. I realize that it is tough to swallow the fact that your actions can cause you to not be blessed on earth or in heaven, but the truth does hurt. **Just as the murderer is held accountable for his murder and the liar for his lies, so will you for your sexual actions**.

For those women who feel they may be too masculine for a man, or the men who feel they may be to feminine for a woman to want them. We should remember that for every sensitive or "soft" man, there is a dominant woman and together they just might work if given a chance. Everything was created for a purpose and we all must work together to make this world revolve at a gentle pace to create harmony. Murder, disease, jail and homosexuality have been chipping away at the base of our families. We need for you to make the right choice and stand on our side and not the side of the enemy.

5.

I AM TALKING TO YOU TOO

For those of you who are reading this and saying, "I'm not a person of color, so this does not affect me," I say, keep reading because I am talking to you too. See we all have a part in this thing from the least to the most, from the first to the last — from the homeless man in the street to the man in the White House. The homeless man has a job to do, a job, which requires him to not give up, nor to give in, but to get up, and keep on going. The man in the White House has a duty to provide for avenues for the homeless man to go down once he gets up. And you, the average white man or woman on the street, have a right to help undo the wrong that you benefit from. There is a difference between "some" and "all". Just because some white people are not racist and hire based on ability, does not mean they all do. We are lulled to sleep by those who do and forget about those who don't. Remember as long as some don't, those of us who do must work together.

Today as a white man you should support not the removal of affirmative action, but instead the reconstruction of the plan. **That's right — you should support Affirmative Action**. I realize the powers that be want you to think that the plan has no place, but the opposite is true. We need the plan more now than ever. The critics say Affirmative Action hurt blacks more than it helped by placing us in positions to fail. Putting companies in uncomfortable positions in which they were forced to promote and hire unqualified blacks. The fact of the matter is, the plan was perfect, but the implementation was poor.

In order to be successful in business, certain steps are needed to build a basis for advancement. You cannot become a manager overnight. At least, you can't become a good manager over night. Affirmative Action forced companies to look at their employees and even more importantly to look at the complexion of these employees. What they found was there were few, if any people of color at any level other than entry level. This created a problem for the company. The law required the numbers, but the companies did not have them. So these companies, in a last ditch effort promoted and hired any and all people who fit the color requirement – Black's were promoted without the benefit of the logical progression of telemarketer to sales associate to outside sales representative to manager. The person now went from telemarketer to manager. The reason for the problem goes back to before the law. If companies had been hiring and promoting blacks from the beginning, they then would have had sales representatives to pull from to place in management positions instead of rushing people along. This rush to fill spots created a whole new challenge for people of color. The so-called black person was forced to either stand on moral ground by turning down this once-in-a-lifetime opportunity, or to press on realizing the challenge of the situation by accepting the promotion. As people of color, we have been overlooked, and the glass ceiling has stood between blacks and the top of the ladder for far too long. The ability to make salaries associated

with these positions has eluded us for so very long, how now
are we to say no? What logic would provide us with a premise
for such a decision? The lack of experience, the lack of knowledge combined with a lack of support from our peers in the
company made up the basis of our decisions. For blacks, this
was the dilemma.

This was the situation when Affirmative Action was
created. The truth of this matter is that Affirmative Action
should have required companies to put a plan in place not for
the promotion of people of color, but for the advancement of
people of color. As a white man right now, you might say:
"No one is putting laws in place to guarantee me the right to
advance. No one is making sure that I have a fair shot at a
job. Affirmative Action discriminates against me." That is
not only a good question, but also a fair question. For that
question I have this answer:

The relationship between blacks and whites is similar
to running a race. Right now, the white man is killing the so-
called black person in this race. In fact, to use laps as a point
of reference. The white man is at least four laps ahead of us.
Four laps ahead is how I see the status of the race today. Lets
look at the race as a whole. In my opinion, the race between
the races is being run like this: In the beginning, the black
man and the white man were at the starting line together.
Stretching, preparing to run the race. Prior to the start of the
race, the great Gods of the game changed the rules. Instead of
racing equally, the white man was told to get on the black
man's back. The great Gods of the game felt this might make
it more interesting. So, for the first two laps, the black man
carried the white man around the track. At the end of these
two laps, the white man got off of the black man's back. They

both prepared to finish the race, but before they could take a step, the great Gods of the game decided that instead of the black man continuing on from there, he would go back to the starting line and run from there. In spite of the fact that now the white man had a two-lap head start. The great Gods of the game still demanded that the black man not only finish the race, but that he catch and attempt to pass the white man. This is why as a white man you should support Affirmative Action. In fact, as a white person, you should support any and all efforts to make the races equal. You should support it because right is right and wrong is wrong. It is wrong for us to be expected to obtain the same level of wealth, education and advancement when you benefited from our service. We are the reason you are where you are today. Just as a wife is entitled to support after a divorce, just as she helped him become what he is today, so does the white man owe the black man, for making him what he is today? If ever there was a divorce, I believe we had it. They say divorce is like war, but for us it took a war.

The black man helped build America from the ground up. We not only helped to dig the ditches, pick the cotton, and construct the homes; we defended this country during times of war. We did all of this, and we did it for free. The white man was able to create companies and gain large sums of money on plantations by utilizing free labor. He used our bodies to build his families homes, our women to raise his children, and when things became tight, he sold us to create cash flow. As I talk to white folks, it amazes me how many of them have rich grandparents or great grandparents. They brag about the money they have and the houses they own. These riches came from somewhere. Somewhere like their parents and grandparents. White people forget the past in an attempt to support the present. In the past, the white man stole many of the ideas created by blacks. They took the ideas and sold them or promoted them for large financial gains. White people as late as the 1960's would steal land from black families. Any land, which was considered profitable or just plain nice to live on, would be taken. The family that lived there would be tormented until they were forced to leave, or be killed. Many in fact were killed because they refused to leave.

This is the role of the white man in history. It is left out of the history books. They promote what they choose to and destroy what they choose to. I'm talking to you when I say that if you claim to be on the side of right, it is your duty to help right the wrongs in your reach. These wrongs have taken place and continue to exist. Never give a man a handout for free, but always give him the path to be free. Without economic stability we can never be free. The system today will never work as long as we let those who once killed and murdered us make decisions. Men who were willing to hang a man while they stood there posing so their friends could take a picture as if they caught a fish. The book entitled Without Sanctuary: Lynching Photography in America by James Allen provides us with vivid pictures of the actions of whites in the early 1900's. Whites would actually make post cards of the lynching to send to family and friends. In these pictures the faces of those involved in the murders are clear to see. These men would chase us down like animals just for the fun of it, burn down our homes while our kids were still in them, and beat our women and elderly men just because they wanted to vote. These are the men who were in their twenties and thirties in the sixties and seventies. These are the men who are in there fifties and sixties now. They now own companies and make hiring and firing decisions. These are the men who we are depending on to make the right decisions when it comes to giving a person of color a fair chance. I know, don't tell me—they have changed?

6.

DOLLARS AND SENSE

Corporate America is based on dollars and cents. The actions and reactions of people influence the future. In order to make it in corporate America, you must (as a man) wear a suit, tie and appropriate shoes. However, the measure of man is not his suit. It is, however, for most women as they evaluate the style of shoe and amounts of heel left. They evaluate the type of tie and silk of which it is made, the brand of suit, and frequency of which it is worn. What I would like for women to see is men is no different, now matter how bad you would like to believe it. We judge you as we see you, and then as you influence our other senses. How many women really care what Tyson (the model) really thinks about peace in the Middle East or what his views are on world hunger? Every women I know thinks he is the greatest and they have never heard him speak. They don't want him to run their companies, they want him as their man. The same thing is true for men. If you really want us to evaluate you on your abilities and potential to perform the job, then don't present yourself as something else. Professional dress for women is still required and can still be done. A woman can be professional and still be sexy. I know this because I see my wife do it daily.

My wife is as fine as the day is long. She has beautiful skin with great features and she has a body that won't quit. She is blessed in the chest and she's got it to show down below. However, she never dresses in a fashion to bring attention to her womanly features no matter how endowed they may be. She knows how to look gorgeous and sensuous without showing the whole world what she's got. She has always been well respected on her jobs and seen as a woman of morals, beauty and intelligence. Men flirt with her because she looks good and her co-workers admire her because she knows her stuff — that's the way it should be. Today we have many women who come to work with something tight on their backside and their entire chest hanging out and wonder why they can't be the managers of the department.

Black women have it really bad about wearing ten earrings, rings on all their fingers and multicolored nail polish to work with gold streaks in their hair and half their butt showing. You are already working against the status quo by being black — why add to it by just dressing the part of a ghetto girl. It will take people twice as long to see you as the educated and competent sister you are. Dress the part and act the part. Just because you like music does not mean that you need to have it blasting at work. Your job is a place for you to provide for yourself and your family with the salary it generates. Don't place your desire to be ethnic over your desire to succeed on your job. Then there is the other side of the coin — the sister who just does not care about perception so she shows up to work or at the grocery store in her house shoes. If your feet hurt, get some comfortable shoes. Stop fooling yourself at the shoe store and buy those size eight shoes instead of the six. You all know who I'm talking about — the sister who wears her curlers outside like they are a hat. She's the sister who ended casual day at work because she wore stretch pants and a halter shirt on Monday and a warm-up suit on Tuesday. If any of this applies to you, this has got to stop. Does this mean you must lose your identity? Of course not, but this does mean you will play the game and follow the rules so you can win and form your own version of the game. Remember, these are the white mans' companies in which you are working and they employ you. You cannot make them accept you, but they can make you accept them. They won't fire you or ask you to change; they will simply continue to overlook you for promotions and allow the white girl to get $2.00 more per raise than you for the same work.

Black men, move away from the trends of society and lean towards the actions, which provide you with success. You already have enough stacked against you because you are black. Do not give them any additional reasons to hold you back or over-look you altogether. Business dress does not include exceptions for you simply because you are black. How do you think the white man sees you when you present yourself in a bright colored suit with a multi-colored tie and an earring? You can say to yourself, "I am not Tomin (acting white) for anyone. If they don't like it forget them." Well you must realize that this is their company and they control who gets promoted and who does not. They have every right to tell you what style of dress is considered appropriate, and until you get your own thing you really have no right to complain. This premise is as old as your daddy saying," As long as you live in my house you will abide by my rules ".

It has always been funny to me how we as people of color feel it is our right to demand certain treatment from white people just because we have chosen to work for them, or because we buy a product they produce we want to make demands on the producer.

It's almost like the U.S. requesting the Japanese treat us a certain way just because we buy their cars. The U.S. did do that, and the Japanese agreed to make some changes, but surprisingly enough the U.S. has seen no progress. See, the Japanese, like the companies in the U.S., have only done enough to keep America quite and to maintain the steady flow of cars being sold to the U.S. The fact of the matter is the Japanese are making a killing off of the U.S. from the sale of cars, electronics and basic labor, and the U.S. gets very little in return. The U.S. provides the Japanese with military protection from all foreign invaders for free and the Japanese still give the U.S. nothing. For all intense and purposes, black folks are the U.S. and the Japanese are white folks. They stole our land, our ideas, our freedom, and today they continue to take our athletic ability, finances and ideas. They take our services and our money and give us very little in return. They allow us to work within their companies, making less money for the same tasks. We continue to be overlooked for promotions to any position of true significance.

They make us managers under the pressures of affirmative action and they give us the position of VP or partner, but they don't give us any power or decision-making ability. Do you really believe they are glad to have you there? White America is fighting you every step of the way in court and through legislation. They are opposed to hire or promotions based on color. It is so unbelievable how white Americans can openly oppose the practice of color based hiring when this is what they do daily. Corporate America was built on referrals of friends and the promotions of family members.

Every now and then you may see a manager or supervisor, but these are normally people who have been there so long or were so overly qualified it was easy to promote them. The real question is when was the last time you saw a black V.P. or President?

All persons who are opposed to Affirmative Action need to remember what the process was like when they interviewed for a job in the past — after you get past the screening of "resumes" and the first interviews, after it comes down to one or two people. This is when affirmative action really shows its stuff. At this point is when the racism that hurts is really carried out. This takes place so often we don't even realize its true effects. The interviewer looks for reasons to hire one person over another. We are talking about those situations where two candidates are close. The white candidate went to Harvard and graduated with 4.0; the Black candidate went to Grambling and graduated with a 4.0. They both have excellent experience and would fit well into the job, so what is the interviewer to do? Find the one, which would provide a better fit within the company. Here is where the black man or woman does not have a chance. The questions go like this:

Interviewer-"So, Mr. White, where did you grow up?"

Mr. White- "On the north side of town in a section called Highland Park. My neighborhood was called Highland Park. I lived around the corner from the high school."

Interviewer-"Is that right? I use to play golf near there on Preston."

Mr. White- "I am familiar with the course—in fact my dad is a member."

Interviewer-"Many of the guys here play there on weekends; maybe you could join us."

Mr. White-"I would really like that."

Interviewer-"Well, other than golf what do you participate in when you have spare time?"

Mr. White- "I enjoy snow skiing and swimming to keep in shape."

Interviewer-"Boy, I wish I had more time to ski because I love it. My parents have a summer home in Denver with a heated in door pool. It's funny that you enjoy swimming, because I swim two miles every morning to relax."

Mr. White –"Boy, that sounds great! At our frat house we swam every day before class."

Interviewer-"A pool in the frat house! Lucky you. What fraternity was that?"

Mr. White- "Sigma Nu."

Interviewer- "Sigma Nu. I was a Gamma Delta and we were always partying with the Sigma Nu's. They were great guys."

Well, you get the idea. This goes on and on with the two of

them meeting on various points of common ground, but with Mr. Black things don't go quite as smoothly.

Interviewer-"Well, Mr. Black, where did you grow up?"

Mr. Black-"I grew up in south Dallas near the old gas station. I attended South O'Cliff high school."

Interviewer- "Oh, really. Well, what do you like to do in your spare time?"

Mr. Black – "I am very active in my church and I enjoy playing basketball on the weekends. Do you like basketball?"

Interviewer- "Well, I really have never been much for it, but I enjoy swimming. Do you swim?"

Mr. Black-"Well, not exactly, see when I was younger, swimming pools were few and far between so I never learned to swim, but I would like to learn."

Interviewer-"Well, Mr. Black, I see here that you were a member of a fraternity in college. I was as well. Which one did you join?"

Mr. Black-"I am a member of Kappa Alpha Psi."

Interviewer-"I don't think I have ever heard of them—were they local?"

Mr. Black-"No, it's a black fraternity, but we have chapters all over the United States. Our primary focus is within the inner city. We initiate programs to help under privi-leged youth."

Interviewer-"I see."

At this point the interviewer has to decide who would be a better fit for the office. Since the office is composed of white men and women ranging in age from 30-60, and they are conservative and not much for change, who do you think he will choose? This, no matter how it may look, is not fair. The White man won because as a white man he will most likely have more things in common with other white men, just as most black people have more things in common with each other. The office will never become more integrated until more blacks are hired, and more blacks won't be hired until they are a better fit. The funny thing is, we are trying to get into their companies so we can invent products for them to sell or to improve the level of service they provide. The true solution rests in us creating and supporting our own stuff. Right now the U.S. is losing jobs left and right as companies move to Japan and Mexico. For this scenario black Americans are the U.S. and the white man is Japan. We have no control because we control nothing. If we want shoes that appeal to our people then we need to start a shoe factory. If we are tired of buying bread from the Chinese store on the corner because they treat us like crap and won't hire blacks, then open your own bread shop and stop giving them your money. The only reason they are open is because of you, and they don't appreciate you, so stop supporting them. In America today we act as if we are so weak and without control, but the fact of the matter is we are in a position to control it all. Money is power, and now we have the money to gain the power. This power comes from all of us using our dollars for the good of

those who care. We have no malls in our neighborhoods, so
we drive to the white neighborhoods and spend our money
there, building up the economic base of that area and doing
nothing for ours. We have no corporations in our area, so we
drive to the white side of town for a job. While we are there
we eat lunch, we buy gas for our cars, and stop at the conven-
ience store to buy a cup of coffee. All day long we build up
their economic base and do nothing for ours. Although I realize they'll give to there own charities and have different foun-
dations they support, there is no one place we all provide
support to. We need to join our resources for one common
goal.

Singers, songwriters, football players, actors, actresses, basketball players, boxers, TV personalities, comedians, track
and field, models, congressmen and women, corporate ex-
ecutives and baseball players — Within these occupations
alone lies enough financial strength to change our condition.
The money these people generate is more than enough to create factories and companies for our own employment. What's
missing is the sense. We do not have enough sense to pull our
resources together. We are too busy competing with each other
when we are not even the competition. Just think about the
names that fall into these categories:

>Bill Cosby, Michael Jordan, Whoopi Goldberg,
>Michael Jackson, Janet Jackson, Whitney Houston,
>Oprah Winfrey (a great example of taking control
>of her life), Michael Johnson, Magic Johnson,
>Emmit Smith, James Earl Jones, Ken Griffey Jr.,
>Quincy Jones and so forth and so on....

* Many of these people already contribute to black organiza-
tions and interest groups.

The list goes on and on and on. I have not even begun to scratch the surface of sports, business or movies. We have more resources than you can a shake a stick at, but when you look around we have nothing. When you need something done. When you need a favor, you go through a white man. When Spike Lee first started, he went to the white man. When rap first came out, they had to go to the white man to get a record deal. It's a shame that we don't have our own. God blesses the child who's got his own. Right now, if you need a house loan or you need a new car loan, the buck stops at the white man's desk. The combined income of the names I have listed above is more than most third world countries, and I only listed twelve names. If we could get everyone to contribute based on a system of giving, we could form our own economic base. If every one making more than one million dollars would contribute as follows:

Annual Income	**Donation**	**Frequency**
1 Million dollars	20,000	every ten years
2-5 Million dollars	40,000	every ten years
6-10 Million dollars	500,000	every ten years
11-20 Million dollars	1 Million	every ten years
21+ Million dollars	2 Million	every ten years

Each donation would go directly towards the building or acquisition of companies and creation of banks. All individuals who donated would receive documentation and would be eligible for funds should they fall on hard times financially. Should someone who has donated in the past lose their status, they would be eligible to receive a position within one of the facilities created from the money with a starter bonus to allow them to pay their bills until they receive a steady check. I realize this looks like a lot of money, but if you are making one million dollars per year, what's 20,000 dollars? For you that's a drop in the hat, but for the average black man, that a year's income and a very good job.

7.

IT MUST BE THE MUSIC

A wise man once said, "If you don't stand for something, you will fall for anything." This saying has become apparently true with the Negro. We have permitted everything to enter, run its course and stay for as long as it chooses without a problem. Drugs, alcohol, disease, improper dress, unemployment, unequal treatment, language, and last but not least, music. Music is a window to the soul of its people. As you look at blocks of time throughout history, you will find one common thread — every period was reflected and influenced by its music. In the 60's and early 70's, the theme of music was peace, sexual freedom, carefree spirits and drugs. Every song from the time was based on one if not all of these things. Was it just the music? Well, let's see about that. During this period more children were conceived then during any other period other than the baby boom. This period was also known for its intense indulgence of drugs.

Without question music reflects the needs, heartache and experiences of a generation, but even more importantly it affects those same individuals. During slavery we used music and song to help us cope with the hard times we experienced. All day long in the field, working in the hot sun with a master beating the mess out of us could have done us in.

However, we sang about the rewards awaiting us on the other side. We told each other "everything's gonna be all right" in song. I can guarantee you if we were singing "kill whites before he kills you" or "the next cracker who hits me dies" slavery would not have lasted 244 years. Music effects our moods and our mentalities. Some say there is nothing wrong with a song that simply tells what is going on the world, a song that tells it like it is in the ghettos and back streets of Harlem or southern California. Although this is true, we have gone past a song and turned it in to a broken record. Song after song — that's basically all our young people hear. It has become subliminal. They call each other "nigger" like it's their name just because that's what the rappers do. They look at their girlfriends, sisters and mothers as "bitches" just like the rappers do.

Remember that slavery did not happen overnight. Ten million of us did not go to bed on Monday and wake up on Tuesday in bondage. They took us one at a time. Even when the boat was full of us, they started by catching us one at a time. Music is taking our children one at a time, teaching them that there is no word too bad to say if it rhymes, informing them of the steps required to be known as "hardcore", revealing to them a world of violence and hate that really is unworthy of exposure. As we said earlier, the time period is expressed through the music of the time, but I feel the music influences the expression of the time. Many kids today who are gangsters learned it from someone else. They dress exactly like the rappers on TV, which they have never met. Kids in the richest neighborhoods, miles from crime, dress "hardcore" because they see it on TV. Why in the world should we believe this child, who does not have enough sense to pull up his pants, or cut his hair, has the sense to not pull the trigger on a gun? They are doing everything else just like the rappers they see on TV they dress, talk and walk just like them. Why should they stop there? Why should we believe they won't be influenced enough to follow the behavior. Why should we think they wouldn't kill? I submit to you today, we should believe they will kill, they have killed, and they have done it because they have seen it and heard it described in song. The recent killings at our high schools are no fluke. As children, we dressed like Batman and rode a broom like the Lone Ranger rode his horse. We pretended to fight like our heroes on Saturday night wrestling and cussed like Richard Prior. So why in the world should we believe that the music they hear and the things they see on TV wouldn't influence our kids? Remember what you saw in the 60's and 70's. What do you think they would see if they looked back at the 90's to-day? It's up to us. Stop supporting the rappers who create mess. If they are not creative enough to describe their situation without using disgusting language, they don't deserve to be performing. Anyone can cuss and hold his balls, but a real man or woman performer can be creative. It's time to take a stand for something before we all fall.

8.

BROTHERS AND SISTERS

Brothers and sisters, we really must begin to look at why we do things. In addition to why we do things, we need to also look at the way we do things. Why in the world is it that when we celebrate anything — a party, wedding, barbecue, graduation — we have to start late? It's bad enough we are all going to be late, but it's worse when the people having the event start late. It never fails. If they say 9:00, it won't start till around 10:00 or later. The other day, I went to a friend's house for a birthday party. The party started at 8:00. The invitations said 8:00. I called in advance to confirm and he said 8:00. My wife and I showed up at 8:05 and both him and his wife were still getting dressed. They were still cooking the food and cleaning up the house. They turned out to be in good shape because the rest of the black folks did not get there until 9:30. The fact still remains, the party was <u>supposed</u> to start at 8:00. We have got to start being on time. No one expects much of us because we do not expect much of ourselves. If we all start showing up on time, then people would be forced to start on time. Even better, if we started our events on time then people would come on time. Everyone who was late would miss the show.

I live in Dallas on the outskirts of town. Our church is

in the inter-city, so the drive is a little far. Sometimes on Sunday morning, we go to a white-based church near our house. This keeps us from driving so far every Sunday. The very first time we went, we showed up at 10:30, because they told us services started then. What forgot this was a white church and they really do start on time. When we got there, the parking lot was full and the music was playing. When they say 10:30, they mean 10:30. From now on, every time we go, we get there by 10:00 along with everyone else. This is what we need to do in our community. Start the event on time with whoever is there. If they want to see the show or participate in the event, they will be there on time. Now we as black people have begun to say the letters - "CPT (Colored People's Time)." Any black person who promotes this concept is the enemy. By giving into the very thought that just because you are black you are on a different time schedule is crime to the race. We must work to do away with the negative images instead of reinforcing them. We accept the time frame of our events because we have done nothing to change them. If we show up on time and leave on time, then the people who hold the events will start to change the mode of operation. If you go to church and service is scheduled from 10:30- 12:00, everyone needs to be in their seats by 10:25 and out of their seats by 12:10. Instead, church starts at 10:40 and ends at 2:00. God never said anything about being late. God is symbolic of love and truth. If you want the service to start at 10:30 and end at 2:00, then say so. Don't continue to mislead people by telling them every ten minutes, that they will be out in the next ten minutes when you know they won't be. This is why in the middle of the service, which should be the end, many people get up and leave. They are not walking out on God. They are walking out on you. They have made plans to go to work that afternoon or to go visit family, but because they thought the service would be over they are forced to walk out in the middle. I have no problem with a full day of service devoted to God, but just be truthful. It's plain and it's simple — in addition to starting on time, we need to make sure to end on time.

Increase your knowledge of the world. There is more to life than just Soul Train and Martin. Find out more about the things around you and make efforts to discover more about the things outside of our hood. Read more. Read about Africa to learn your history. The reason why we except the truth the white man have printed is because we don't know the true story. Read to find out how to improve yourself and your status. Read to discover how to be a better man, woman, employee and/or parent. Read to become more than what your are today.

Stop being so selfish. There is more to life than just you. Look at what is important to your friends, family and children. If your parents are in need and cannot provide for themselves, help them out. They were there for you, and now you need to be there for them. Put your spouse above you every now and then. See what her needs are and try to fulfill them. If she doesn't give equally then you two need to talk, but nine times out of ten a good mate will give also. Start your own business and support existing businesses. I am not saying not to go to other businesses owned by whites; this would be foolish. What we need is equality within our own minds. Right now we cater to those white businesses more than we do so-called black ones. We drive past these businesses to get to white ones. This is stupid and hurtful to us. Support your children and the school they attend. It is not the teacher's job to raise your child; it's your job to raise them and their job to teach. Work on your kids at home and provide them with some sense of right and wrong. Don't blame the teacher if your child is undisciplined. The instillation of discipline is your job. The change, if any, must come from us— from the way people see us to the way we see ourselves, from the way our children are seen to the way they see themselves.

9.

SENSE INSTEAD OF STRENGTH

In the days of our forefathers, church was a place where they went for daily advice and motivation. They spent all day long on Sunday in church, praying and asking the Lord to give them strength and to give their children strength. They looked for strength to overcome the hardships that the white man had placed on them and continue to impose upon us. They continued to ask for God to open doors and make a way for them to continue on. Well now, things have changed. We still need the Lord for guidance and direction, but now we need sense verses strength. We need knowledge to overcome the problems and barriers formed in front of us and around us.

The days of church sermons, which began with "He woke me up this morning and started me on my way," which were filled with a lot of yelling, jokes and dancing, have passed us by. Today we need logical direction; we need to know what the bible says in plain English about overcoming the situation. Black people must ask more of themselves today then ever. We have to come out of our shell, our little world where music, clothes, hair and sex are paramount. While we have the latest hair and are creators of the best dances, and can't be touched on the basketball, court we have no working knowledge of the things that count. We need to focus on the progressive topics that will take us into the 21st century and allow us to compete in corporate America. We have no knowledge of the Internet or futuristic technology. Let a movie come out about the future like <u>Star Trek, Star Wars</u> or <u>Men in Black</u>. That theater will be filled with white folks, and although there will be some of us in there (because Will Smith is in it) the majority of us are down the hall watching <u>Booty Call</u> or <u>I'm Gonna Get You Sucka</u>. We must start to think to the future about what direction the world is moving towards. Many of the things that are a reality today at one time were simply ideas in the movies before. Today we live in a world of cloning, laptop computers, cell phones, videophones, and abortion pills. This world is evolving at a rate 1000 times the speed of that which we are use to. In order to keep up, we have to change our focus.

My mother was right when she asked the Lord to give her strength to make it through another day, because back then if you just kept on living things would work out. You could figure out what you would do that day when it came, but today simply being here is not enough. We need a plan for our success, and we need to grow with the plan and pass the plan on to our children. We must expand our horizons to include politics, religion, education and race relations. Right now we have nothing to pass on to our children but broken, unfulfilled dreams — dreams of freedom, dreams of equality, dreams of equal access, dreams of being judged on our character and not the color of our skin. Nothing but dreams has resulted from this speech. I find it sad that in the 200 years since slavery, I still have not identified a true leader of our people since Martin Luther King Jr. Black folks truth is truth. We have been running, ducking and dogging for so long that we don't know any other way. Well, we need to learn another way that involves us standing up and fighting for our rights instead of simply waiting for someone to get tired of kicking our butts and giving it to us. We know what we want — let's carry out the plan by doing our part.

     I realize we don't want to admit it, but the truth of the matter is we had something to do with the length of time we remained slaves. In fact, we had something to with the very capture of blacks when slavery began. When the first slaves were taken from Africa, this action worked like a thief in the night. The white man came, saw, and captured. This, however, was not the way it continued. The white man continued to return with larger boats and more and more people and equipment. Each time the slave traders took more of us captive than the last trip. Word spread like wild fire in Africa about this evil force with white skin, which came in the night and kidnapped that which was in his path. Another sentence also spread- I'm glad it wasn't me. You don't remove hundreds of thousands of people from a location like Africa without people realizing they are missing. The thing was, we were not so concerned with who was being taken, but who was not. The many Africans that were left when the first two thousand slaves were taken must have been concerned with their own existence. If they were truly concerned with those that were taken, they would have taken action. I realize there was a language barrier. Many of the tribes were unable to speak and some were even at war with each other, but something like this requires action. The African people, the African government, never really did anything to prevent the kidnapping of their people.

     After the first four thousand people were taken, the

African people should have been waiting at the ocean shore for the boats to pull ashore with spears and rocks in their hands. They should have had the leader of the greatest tribe standing in the front with a sign in African which said "I wish you mother f-ckers would." The reason why the white man continued to pillage Africa for every asset, which it possessed from gold to silver to its people, was because we let them in without conflict. If we had simply made it tough for them to kidnap and enslave our loved ones, caused them to lose lives to gain slaves, just maybe they would have turned around. They continued because it was easy pickings. Some might say that the United States in a massacre type style, would have killed us, but in the beginning it was not the entire United States that was involved. The slave trade began by the kidnapping of many by a few rogue traders. When they raided the village, we all ran. We ran in different directions and the ones that got caught became slaves and those, which got away said, "yeah at least it was not me."

It is amazing to me how things really have not changed much today. We continue to stand by and watch as white companies take our money but won't employ us; they sell their goods in our neighborhoods without giving back. We pretty much scratch our heads and say at least it was not me. We complain, but never do anything. Slavery stopped due to laws passed by the white government, which really got tired of having us around and kicking our butts. The good white folks won over the evil. The good white folks organized the troops for the civil war. True enough, we fought, but the battle should have occurred one hundred and fifty years ago. A black slave who was tired of getting his butt kicked should have started the battle.

Hear me when I say the black man was not all weak and scared. In fact, many of us were looking for opportunities to be free, but every time a plan came about the person leading it would have trouble getting support because so many of us were afraid to join due to fear of the master's hand (just like today). The few brothers with some heart would put together a minor plan to organize, but it never failed, there was always one brother who was looking to make the master happy or wanted to show the master he could be trusted by rating us out. Then we would all gather in the field while the man made an example of the brothers. We all stood by while two or three white men would hang ten to twenty brothers. Three or four hundred of us would watch. We watched and said, "At least it ain't me." The same things would occur while our husbands, wives sons and mothers were beaten. What is wrong with us? How could we stand by and watch as our loved ones and friends were tortured and killed when we had the numbers?

We always had them out numbered at least 10-1 on any given plantation. They may have had guns, but they can't shoot three hundred of us before we get the five or ten of them. Yes, we allowed slavery to continue by providing a forum for it to succeed. We were good "nigger's" that worked hard and never complained. They told us we were animals, but they had sex with us like humans. They knew. They have always known, but were never willing to disclose it. Black folks remember that. That's where the problems occurred. Because the good white folks chose to no longer live a lie, to no longer go along with actions which were wrong. The good white folks took a stand as strong as the stand taken by the bad white folks. That's right, we would not be free if it were not for those good white folks. Remember that there are good and bad in every race of people, and the teams need to be redefined based on intent and purpose. If you are on the side of right, you are on my team. I don't care what color you are.

10.

OUR PART

Our part is funny for me to say, because for so long we have not really had a part we could feel good about. We have not had a part of history outside of slavery. Our past was thrust upon us without input or regard for truth. Through slavery, we were nothing more than things to be used. In the days of segregation, we were just happy to be semi-free so we took what was left. Today we have to make a conscious choice to change and get involved based on our new role in society. Martin Luther King Jr. once said the dilemma for blacks today is to contribute to society despite the challenges of history, which have been placed upon us. In other words, even though we started out behind, have been held back and continue to be the last hired and the first fired, we still have to be just as productive of those who have never been faced with these hurdles.

Our part involves us having some pride and dignity about ourselves. Remember in the movie <u>Roots</u> when Cunta Kenta was forced to say his name. The master would not stop whipping him until he would say the word Toby. Well, every time a black person collects welfare, he is saying Toby. Every time a black woman sells herself on the street for money, she is saying Toby. Every time a young black man kills another or sells drugs in his own neighborhood, he is saying Toby. Our part involves participation from everyone on our team. All of those who sit in church on Sunday talking about how right they are and all of those public officials who claim to care about the importance of doing right, we need you. We need to separate the good from the bad and the friends from the enemies — first within our race and then within this world.

If you are a male or female person of color between the ages of 18 and 50 and you are able to work, but choose not to in order to get welfare,
> *— It's time to do battle.*

If you belong to a gang which kills simply because this one has on black or that one was has on blue,
> *— It's time to do battle.*

If you have willfully committed a crime against anyone no matter what the circumstance,
> *— It's time to do battle.*

If you are in management, or in a position of influence within your company and you have done nothing to help blacks, but have bent over backwards for whites,
> *— It's time to do battle.*

If you are a drug dealer or benefit from the funds raised from selling drugs,
> *— It's time to do battle.*

If you are a parent who is raising your kids to respect no one, not even you and to dress, talk, and do as they please,
> *— It's time to do battle.*

If you are the one who support the liquor store on the corner, the porno shack or the gun shop,

> *— It's time to do battle.*

If you married a white girl, just because she was white, without giving a sister a chance,

> *— It's time to do battle.*

When I label a person or a group of persons as "the enemy," I am establishing the area of focus. No longer do we need to protect those who hurt us. I am not trying to say that I am perfect or that I have never done anything wrong. In fact, I have made so many mistakes and messed up so many times that I have stopped counting. The difference is that I am not doing those things now. It's not what you have done that count. What truly counts is what you are doing. I do not care if you were in jail, did drugs, beat your wife, drank till you passed out, lived on welfare, purchased pornography, abandoned your kids or practiced homosexuality. None of these things matter. No one is perfect. Like I said, I have done almost everything a man could do, but now I am the man I have always wanted to be. I am the man my family deserves to have. I have not just said I that I wanted to change, I have actually done it. So, for all of the brothers out there who have given up because of their past. For all of the individuals who say, "I can't get a real job, because I have a criminal record". Or for the man who says "I cannot call my child because seven years ago I left them alone with their mother." For all of the people who are not going forward because of the past, I say to you, bull s—t. You are not going forward because of you. You are the reason you dropped out of school, not the child you had. You are the reason you cannot hold a steady job. You are the reason you can't get ahead on your bills. You are your own enemy, and only you can change you. Stop licking your wounds and get up and take control. I realize it is tough when you are continually reminded of your faults. When they throw your past in your face, look right back at them and say, "that was then, and this is now." I don't care what you heard or what you saw me do. I vow now that it will never be done again. This is the new me and I want to be a new creature, but it's up to you; will you let me be the new person I desire? See it's up to us to see the new person once they establish they are changing. If we want them to get off welfare then we must give them a job. If we want them to come home and help in the raising of their children then we must let them in the house. If you will let me, I want to get off of welfare. Remember it starts with them and ends with them; our part is in the middle.

The time has come to get serious with those who have been serious with us. Whenever a person of color is arrested, we run to their defense regardless of guilt or innocence. Then, if they don't get the same sentence as a white man, we get mad. The fact of the matter is they should not have committed the crime in the first place! As long as they receive a fair trial and it is proven that they are in fact guilty, then we should want them to be punished to the full extent of the law. And after the punishment is handed down, we should publicize it to everyone everywhere to let our children know what will happen to them if they commit crimes.

Recently in California a black man was sentenced to life in prison for stealing a piece of fruit. It was his third strike and under the new law the third strike was the last. Black people became upset because of the sentence. Well, I feel the focus should have been on the fact that this was his third crime, and prior to stealing fruit what else did he do? I know he did more than just steal fruit to get placed in jail three times. Never once did he deny stealing the fruit. In my family I have a family member who is in prison for life also. He is in jail under the three strikes and you're out law like this man. His mother who is a very nice person and a loyal parent visits him regularly in his new home (prison). After every visit she tells us about how he should not have been given life for one crime. Although I feel for her and I would not want to be in jail for life. The focus should be on the life that her son has lived. He has always been in trouble and he has been caught committing three crimes by the police. She should still visit him in jail and she should write him letters, but she also should realize he is a criminal who has committed crimes, which require punishment. Just like the homosexual example in chapter five. Look at the action and not the person committing the action. If the action is wrong it does not matter who commits it, it is still wrong.

We should increase the number of brothers who, after committing three crimes, are sent to prison for life. We should take each case and print the details of the three crimes and the sentence they received. This information should be placed in the hands of every black person we can find. We should let them know the law is not fair for you, so don't do the crime. People want you to believe fear does not serve as a deterrent to crime, but in the days of slavery and Jim Crow, you could not pay a black man to run through certain parts of town. There was no way he would steal from certain stores, due to the fear of what the white man would do to them if they were caught. Black folks made it a point not to eat in a white restaurant, drink from white fountains or use their bathrooms (no matter how bad you had to go) for fear of the reaction.

Grown men would use the bathroom on themselves before using the white man's bathroom. Today our children fear nothing and respect even less.

Mothers have given the child the feeling of being untouchable as they proclaim no one touches me! My MOMMA doesn't even touch me. Children will state this to the teacher's face, to the preacher's face and to any other face responsible enough to try to provide direction. The mother who instills this attitude is the enemy. We need a parent to raise a kid who realize when respect, is appropriate.

I agree that if children are being hit for no reason, then action must be taken by the child to get out of the situation. If the teacher is trying to teach and the child is acting up, the teacher must be able to restore order by talking to a child who has received some form of training at home. We have parents (often just the mother) who for some reason find it cute to raise kids who are disrespectful and have not mastered the art of following instruction. Well, if they can't follow home instruction, then they can't follow classroom instruction and they can't follow societal instruction. Thus, they end up dropping out of school or committing some form of crime. Once they commit the crime, the discipline the parent did not want to provide, will be gladly performed by the department of justice. We must take action against the enemies I have listed above with the fury and fight that we would any other white-based opponent, like the KKK. These enemies are worse for the black race then any other because they work to eat us up from the inside out. The white man need not kill us when he can get us to do it for him. He need not drug us when we are willing to take it ourselves. He need not discriminate against us when we won't hire or promote our own brothers and sisters. If it is because we are jealous and don't want to see them out do us. Or maybe we think there is only enough room for one. These internal enemies will breakdown the advancements we make and tear down any unity we may establish. Why do our neighborhoods consist of liquor stores, check cashing places, gun shops and porno shops? These places continue to exist because we continue to frequent them. These places do not exist in many white areas, because they boycott them and bring shame to those who enter. It no longer is lucrative for the owner, so he moves to another spot with less problems and better profit-like our neighborhoods.

In this area more than any other we are our own worst enemy. We act as if we are children without control of our own desires. We act as if just because they build it, we must use it, so we blame the white man for building it. He put it right there on purpose to bring us we down, we proclaim. It's all a part of the plan to bring us down. Eleanor Roosevelt once said, "No one can make you feel inferior without your consent. " Brothers and sisters, they do not control us if we don't allow ourselves to be controlled. Take control of your wants and desires before they take control of you. Let them build what ever they choose. Time has shown us we can't stop them, anyway, but when they do build it, walk by it as if were not there. Refuse to buy a thing or to utilize the service. After a time, they will have no choice but to close up the doors due to lack of revenue.

All members of gangs should be treated as the enemy with a firm plan to destroy them from the inside out. We continue to stand by, stating, "that's my baby, he really is a good kid" or "that's my little girl and she just got in with the wrong crowd." Well, now your baby and little girl are killers and drug dealers and they are destroying our neighborhoods and the good kids within. These individuals are holding people captive in their own homes.

You go to our neighborhoods and you see bars all over the windows and doors. We have dogs in the backyard for protection and wire across the tops of our fences because of the fear your little boy and baby girl has instilled. The white man, on the other hand, lives free of the fear we impose on ourselves with his windows free of bars, his doors free of bars and the dog he has is a pet and not a security guard. Why is this? Why does this continue? Why do we allow this to happen? We don't react because we wait for someone else to. Those of us with money move away to the white neighborhoods so we can live free of bars, jog in our neighborhoods without fear, let our kids play in the street or at the park. I tell you this is a shame that we are living like this because of ourselves. Just because the white man allows guns to flow through our neighborhoods like water does not mean we must use them. A gun with no one to pull the trigger is nothing but metal. Drugs without anyone to sell them or take them are harmless, but as long as we continue to act like fools who don't have the sense to control ourselves, then we will continue to be victims. As long as we keep doing what we are doing we will keep getting what we got. Believe it or not, the brothers we run from are our own people. We have now become the enemy.

The bars are meant to keep them away and to keep us secluded from the threat they represent, but just as the white man can't run from the situation they have created, neither can we. Our fates and lives are all intertwined and our destinies related. No one will be freed from his or her prisons as long as the black man stays trapped in his.

THE BEGINNING
(For anyone willing to change)

About the Author

Frank S. does not fit the mold of typical creators of such types of works. Frank was raised in a single-family household with his brother and half sister. His father, a janitor from South America, left the family when Frank was only six years old. His mother, an immigrant from Guyana who never completed high school, often worked as many as three jobs to support the family. While his mother worked, Frank and his siblings were left to discover the world for themselves. As a result of imposed school bussing, Frank found himself in a world of prejudice and racism that seemed to have no boundaries. He found blacks that looked down on him due to his clothes, dark skin and financial status, and he found whites that looked down on him because they could.

After a lifetime of dealing with racism, Frank decided to take control of his life through individual control and improvement. Frank attended New Mexico State University on a football scholarship, and later went on to graduate with a degree in Sociology. Upon graduation he began his professional career as a sales representative. As a result of hard work and focus, Frank is now the highest-ranking person of color for a major pharmaceutical company. Frank has made the removal of racism a primary focus in his life. He feels that the truth truly can set America free. He also feels that he is the right person to tell that truth. This book will elicit controversy and flames of anger from Americans both black and white, but Frank feels he has the armor to withstand the heat.

www.ingramcontent.com/pod-product-compliance
Lightning Source LLC
Chambersburg PA
CBHW030028290326
41934CB00005B/536